Marin

Rhyme *Time*

Original
Story Poems

For Children
of All Ages

By
John Marinelli

Rhyme *Time*

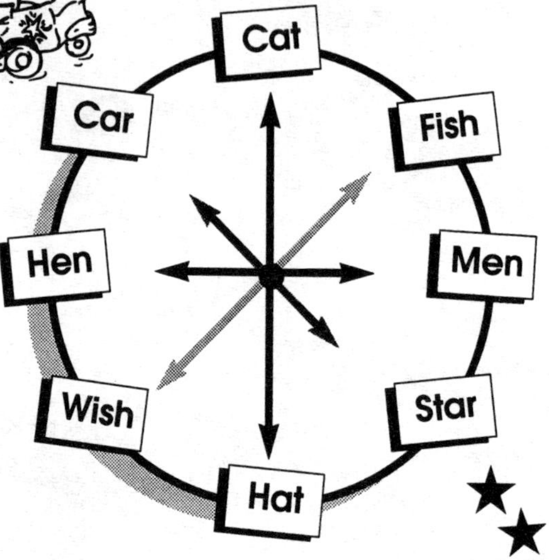

Rhyme Time may be purchased for education, sales promotional or fund raising use. All profits from fund raising sales will be used for the Bless the Children Project, and Out Reach of Marinelli Ministries. For information please write:

Marinelli Ministries, Box 341, Ponte Vedra Beach, Fl 32004

Library of Congress Catalog Card Number: 96-94055
ISBN 1-57502-137-4

Printed in the USA by

MORRIS PUBLISHING
3212 E. Hwy 30
Kearney, NE 68847
800-650-7888

Acknowledgements

This book is the result of my wife's ongoing love and support as she encouraged me to share my poetry with others. For this I am deeply greatful. Marilyn also selected and drew art for use in this book.

Additional thanks goes to Janice Long who typeset the pages and completed the final layouts including design and the second cover.

Special thanks to my mother, Mrs. Lois Marinelli and Ronnie Long for proof reading.

To God be the glory for the inspiration and where-with-all to make this happen.

Table of Contents

Table of Contents

About The Author

Rev. Marinelli is a Bible Teacher, Christian Playwrite and Poet. He is a sales representative for an industry publisher and father of two grown children. He and his wife Marilyn are Christians who believe in Faith as the source of answered prayer, Hope as the key to a happy future and Jesus Christ as the only way to God's eternal love.

The children's poems were written in story form for expressive reading by Parents, Grandparents and other story tellers. It is the poets hope that "Rhyme Time" will be used to invoke laughter, joy and other feelings of life in the lives of children everywhere.

What time is it? **Its Rhyme Time ...**

Time to share a story with a child, and capture a smile while passing through the day.

The Beauty of a Rhyme

Have you ever tried to read a rhyme
at a most inopportune time?
When no one wants to hear
especially those who are near?

When the beauty of the rhyme
doesn't fit the present time?
And when the listeners do not care
that's almost too much to bear.

It's a real joy to fashion a rhyme,
how sad that the world has no time.
For in the beauty of a rhyme
lies a feeling or a thought for to find.

So for the poet and his rhyme,
please – try to find some time.
The joy that will come your way
could last forever or just for today.

Let's Catch A Fish

Let's take a dish
and catch a fish
in the pond down below.

We'll cut a hole
and slide our dish
through the ice and snow.

But if our dish
does not catch a fish
in the pond down below,

We can still jump and play
until the end of day,
then off for home we'll go.

Max

There once was a lumberman named Jack
who had a little friend called Max.
Now Jack roamed the forest wide
with Max always at his side.

He lived at the bottom of an old oak tree
which faced the edge of a deep blue sea,
and Max lived there too,
ever since he left the zoo.

Jack was a lumberman
who had a mighty right hand,
and when he swung his trusty ax
there at his side was little Max.

But then one day when the work was done
Jack looked around but Max had run.
Gone from his master's side,
gone to roam the forest wide.

So Jack went back to his house by the sea
to wait for Max to return from his destiny,
for he no longer could swing his ax
without the presence of his little friend Max.

A Poet Without A Rhyme

In a time that was way back when
    where words were fashioned by famous men,
there was a poet of a kind
    a man who sought to fashion a rhyme.

He felt the sway of a gentle breeze
    as children played in falling leaves.
He saw the beauty of the sea
    but could not capture its majesty.

He knew the poets from other lands
    their words were read by many fans.
But, as a poet without a rhyme
    he found no fame in his own time.

But that didn't stop this poet to be
    he sought and searched and looked to see.
What was the secret of the rhyme
    money?, fame?, or just a good time?

As a poet without a rhyme
    he failed the test of time.
But now he writes in eternity
    fashioning words that are to be.

If I Were a Tree

If I were a tree, I'd fill the sky
for all to see and wonder why.
I'd shade the world on a hot summer's day
and beckon to all who pass my way.

I would sway in a gentle evening breeze
and change the season with falling leaves.
I would offer a branch to a feathered friend
and grant a kiss to the howling wind.

I would be there come rain or shine
down through the ages till the end of time.
I would stand tall for all to see,
that is ... if I were a tree.

Who Could It Be?

Who makes the thunder and the rain
Who feeds the buffalo their grain
Who cares for the fish in the sea
And hatches the egg that houses the flea?

Who teaches the lion's cub to play
And brings the night to cover the day
Who showed the birds how to fly
Who gave me wisdom to question why?

Who formed the stars that shine in the night
Who do we thank for the joys of life
Who designed the worlds and made eternity
I wonder who, who. Who could it be?

An Elephant Named Clyde

There once was an elephant named Clyde
who had a tummy that was so very wide.
Now Clyde lived in the jungle deep
he loved to eat and especially to sleep.

All the other animals laughed at Clyde
because his tummy was so very wide.
But Clyde didn't seem to care
he just slept in the warm summer air.

All of a sudden one very hot day
when all the animals were hard at play,
Clyde sniffed danger in the air
he called to his friends, "Beware! Beware!".

Out of the heat of a hot, hot day
a raging fire came to stop their play.
Mr. Lion ran to hide, and
Mrs. Moose sat down and cried.

But all the other animals gathered around
to watch Clyde as he cleared the ground.
For with his tummy that was so very wide
Clyde cleared a path from side to side.

Then with a very loud roar
Clyde sprayed water at the fires door,
he opened a path for all the see
and everyone dashed to a place of safety.

So the elephant named Clyde
whose tummy was so very wide,
became the hero of the day
and now is included when it's time to play.

The Little Blue Car

There once was a little blue car
who thought that he was a movie star.
A proud little car was he
for he was happy and he was free.

Free to dart and dash beside the sea,
just to be what ever he wanted to be.
We tried to tell him he was just a car,
and not really a Hollywood movie star.

But you know how that is
trying to talk to a little blue whiz,
he would laugh and then just say
that stuff is not for me today.

I am a movie star and not just a little blue car
I am going to travel some day and I'll go far.
He sure looks like a little blue car,
but you know, maybe he really is a star.

Snowball

There once was a cat so bright and fluffy.
A cute little cat, but sometimes rather huffy.
We love her anyway
and pet her everyday.

She drinks from the water tap,
strange, that little cat.
She likes to climb way up high
and then look down with a gentle sigh.

She curls up at the end of our bed
every time there's something to be said.
She'll even play with our hair
just to let us know she's there.

She waits patiently at the door,
till we return from work or the store.
She bathes herself every single day
for that's her life ... that's her way.

She sleeps on the top of our TV set,
calm, assured and without a single fret.
She thinks she is the family mother,
now that's really funny brother.

She'll run from door to door
checking on the kids and even more.
She's the cat that sits in the hall
she's our sweetheart, our little snowball.

Sue

I've searched the whole night through
    hoping to find my lost lovely Sue.

But now she has gone away
    lost in my dreams of yesterday.

And now I am all alone, sad and blue
    thinking of the times I had with Sue.

She was a joy to all around
    at times she was even a clown.

But now my Sue is nowhere to be found,
    Gee, how I loved that old hound.

The Three Little Grumps

Once upon a time
there were 3 little grumps
who had nothing to say.

They followed each other
all around the house
in a pouting sort of way.

Mumble! Grumble!
From grump to grump
there echoed a sigh.

Boo! Hoo!
They said aloud
with a great cry.

Oh how sad
were the three little grumps
that slowly passing day.

There was nothing
for them to do
and no one wanted to play.

So the three little grumps
joined in a row
bottom lip to the ground.

Until they were
all grumped out
ending the day with a frown.

The Fish Without A Tail

Once there was a fish without a tail
who swam by the use of a sail.
Across the oceans wide
sailed the fish in all his pride.

One day he came across a whale
who said, "how strange you have no tail".
But the fish with the sail for a tail
gently smiled at this friend the whale.

Then he said with a hearty reply,
"how strange that you should wonder why"?
For a fish without a tail
could never swim without a sail.

So the fish without a tail
said goodbye to his friend the whale
and swam away by the use of his sail.

The Little Chicken
(A True Story)

A story for you
a story for me.
This is a story of a little chicken
who once sat on my knee.

With his feathers ruffled and his eyes so bright,
the little chicken soared in the midst of flight
around the barn and beyond the tree
flew the little chicken back to my knee.

A bond of love so true you see
between the little chicken and me.
I watched him grow and splash and play.
It seemed that the little chicken was here to stay.

But then one day when I came home from play
the little chicken wasn't there that day.
I sought and searched and looked to see
what had happened to the little chicken
who once sat on my knee.

With a saddened heart and tears in my eyes
I came to the supper table to find a surprise
There in my plate, I learned the fate
of the little chicken who we all ate.

The Dog with a Waggly Tail

Once upon a barefoot trail
appeared a dog with a waggly tail.
With a bark and a very loud growl
he always chased the man with the mail.

Across the fields and down the lane
ran the man the way he came.
For the dog with the waggly tail
chased the man who carried the mail.

Then one hot and sunny day,
the mail man stopped to say,
"Mister dog with a waggly tail
for you today, I have some mail".

Now the dog with the waggly tail
likes the man who carries the mail,
together they walk along the way,
delivering the mail most every day.

Mr. Peek-A-Boo

Mister Peek-A-Boo
peeked the whole day through.
Around the corners wall
through the trees that stood so tall.

He sneaks a peak or two
always searching for a clue.
With his watchful eye
He looks for reasons why.

Look out for Mister Peek-A-Boo,
one day he might peek at you.

Let's Make a Memory

Let's make a memory
that will last a long long time.
Let's make a memory
and record it in this rhyme.

Together we'll soar like a bird
far above the clouds.
Then dive to the ground
and walk as men among the crowds.

We'll be the white polar bear
who lives in the zoo.
How about taking an old boat
and make it all brand new?

It's fun to pretend
go ahead and create the scene
Do it with mom and dad.
It's okay to shape your dream.

The Silly Poem

Me said two or was it three
and five ran and hid behind a tree
Then it rained in my shoe.
Oh my! What shall I ever do?

Six multiplied by the power of four
and seven, eight, nine out the door.
Then it rained again in my shoe.
Oh my! What shall I ever do?

Ten divided twice by no more
takes eleven and twelve to the store.
Then it rained again in my shoe.
Oh my! What shall I ever do?

Then one said or was it three
two times five sets everyone free.
Then it rained in my other shoe.
Oh my! What shall I ever do?

Candy K-9 Critter

There once was a collie
who was very pretty.
She plays with her bone,
and sometimes with the kitty.

She sits on command
to give me her paw
then runs off to play
with something she saw.

She's my K-9 critter
a joy to have around.
The pick of any litter
always alert to every sound.

Candy collie dog to see
a gift from God above.
Roll over, sit down, come to me
full of joy and love of love.

The Value of a Dream

Once upon a sleepless night,
I gazed at a passing star
and pitched a dream to travel far.

Through my mind and into the air
soared a thought and a care.
Up into a blue-gold sky
sailed my dream so very high.

Some laughed at my dream
others were cruel and mean.
Yet I knew it would answer its call,
for I pitched a thought that wasn't small.

Should my dream really come true,
and the thought I pitched get through.
They who laughed and were so mean,
will truly see the value of a dream.

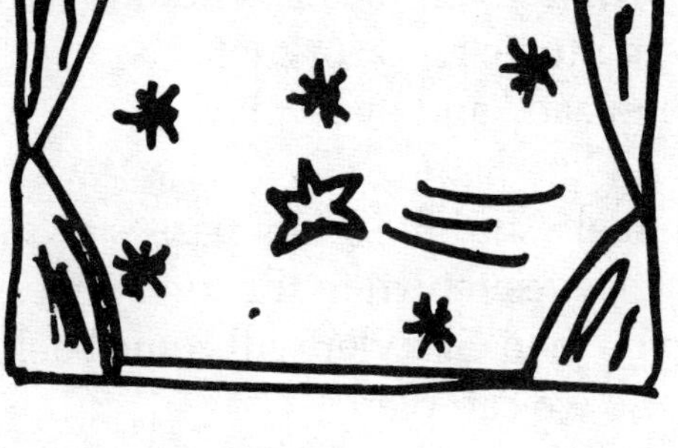

Two Shoes

There once was an Indian boy
whose name was Two Shoes.
He lived in a village by the sea.

Two Shoes loved to fish and play
Especially with his little friend Growler.
They were foot loose and fancy free.

But then one cold day
when the village moved from the sea
Two Shoes realized that Growler had run away.

"Where did he go?" said Two Shoes
as he wiped the tears from his eyes.
"Will my friend, Growler, ever come back to play?"

Little Deer laughed with a deep voice
causing his Tepee to dance with sound.
Then he said, "I know where Growler might be."

Winter is coming and it's time to sleep
Growler is probably off in search of a cave
You'll find him in the spring over by the sea.

But Growler was my very best friend
this is going to be hard for me.
I'll wait for him each and every day.

When the ice melts and the snow passes away
When the leaves return to the forest trees
Maybe then Growler will come back
so we can play.

Ratter Chatter Chat

In the ratter of his chat
appeared a chatter like a rat
His chatter was so fat
that they called him Ratter Chatter Chat.

His caty chattering like a rat
echoed throgh the night until it sat.
Everyone knew that it was Ratter Chatter Chat
that made the chatter like a rat.

Ratter Tatter went his chat
caty chattering like a rat
For that's the ratter of his chat
and why he's called Ratter Chatter Chat.

The Doodle Poem

A Rink, A Dink, A Doo
many more and few.
Now that's a real kadu
without the hooty who.

Beatly Weathly Twee
ankle to the knee.
Hurrah! Hurrah! for me
all about life's tree.

Tweetly Deetly Dum
in a barber nickle's fun.
A Tootle, Tootle Dee
For one and all to see.

The Diddy-Bop

There once was a Diddy-Bop
who bopped the day away
with fancy shoes and twinkle toes
He bopped and bopped most every day.

Daddy-Bop said "What's into Diddy
that he should Bop! Bop! all day?"
But Lady-Bop just smiled and said,
"Listen to what Diddy has to say."

So Diddy rose up to Bop-A-Rue-Bop
as everyone looked on with glee
Then Diddly suddenly came to a stop
and said, "This is what's happening to me."

I saw the Bop in the Bop-A-Shoe-Bop
and it felt good to my soul.
So I filled up my shoe with lots of Bop
and now I can Shoe-Bop the stroll.

Diddy-Bop! Diddy-Bop Diddy Bop-Bop
I am the Diddy with a Bop
Ready to Bop-A-Shoe-Bop
Until there's no more Bop.

The Skutch

There once was a skutch
who went from door to door
with too many questions
spitting out words galore.

"Go away!" said I, said I
peaking through my window glass.
"I've no time for questions
or words that last and last.

Onward she comes
down my narrow walk
with nothing more in mind
than to talk, and talk, and talk.

"Oh!" says I, says I
as at my door she knocks.
The Skutch has finally arrived
to put peace upon the rocks.

Hello my Little Skutch
good bye my day of rest.
Speak on Little Skutch
and I'll answer with my best.

My Barnyard Friends

"Moo" spoke the old Cow
while Little Piggy Pig looked on
But Ms. Sassy Duck swam away
Quacking out her own little song.

Then old Donkey Doo said "Hee Haw!!"
as the sun shined over the day
These are my barnyard friends
who rose up early to play.

Out to pasture they went
off to spend the time
Quacking and oinking and moo-ing away
In a funny sort of rhyme.

"Moo" went that old Cow, "Moo! Moo!"
But Piggy Pig fell into the mud with glee
as Mr. Donkey Doo said, "Hee Haw! Hee Haw!
and the ducks swam across the pond to see.

Now the day was far spent
It was time to return from play.
To settle down for the night,
until the light of the next glorious day.

Seven Little Frogs

Seven little frogs
leaped into my yard
just to say "Hello"!

One leaped over another
up and down, all around
as I wondered where they'd go,

Across the yard
and down the path
they played their game.

Hopping and jumping
and leaping all day
suddenly to leave as they came.

Around the barn
and beyond the tree
they hurriedly go.

Back to the lillies
and safety of the night
to the pond down below.

The Cat and the Rat

I once matched a cat with a rat
and put them in a magical hat.
there in the depths of my hat,
sat the cat and the rat.

"A hocus pocus, I did say
a pinch of salt and a Hay! Hay! Hay!"
then with my magical wand
I formed a brand new bond.

With my magic and my hat
I matched a cat with a rat,
and to my awful surprise
that thing began to rise.

It leaped onto the floor
then it growled or did it roar?
It wasn't a cat and it wasn't a rat
whatever it was, there it sat.

I wondered what I had done
as I watched it hop, or did it run?
Well I put up my magic and my hat
and said good bye to the cat and the rat.

Little Boy Tuffy

So rough and tough was he
    that I could not even raise my knee.
I'll bet he's too tough for you
    I know he's too tough for me.

They call him "Little Tuffy"
    and he belongs to me.
I tickle his toes and he ganks my nose
    we fall on the floor and on it goes.

I've got you and you've got me
    whose got who, says we.
With a growl and a roar and a kick in the air
    I try to get up and he yells, "No Fair"

He is my Little Boy Tuffy
    rough and tuff and sometimes huffy.
But its all in fun each day
    as a little boy and his dad laugh and play.

Old Mister Owl

I once made a friend of a feathered fowl,
he called himself "Old Mister Owl".
For he was very very wise
even though he was half my size.

Old Mister Owl lived in a tall oak tree
right next door to Mr. and Mrs. Honey Bee.
His nest was made of sticks and lots of straw
but most of the time he slept on the top of a car.

We were friends, the owl and me
both of us were wild and free,
to dash through the open fields
or just to play by the moon lit sea.

I sure love that old owl
even when he began to growl.
Boy was I surprised to hear
a growl, as Old Mister Owl flew near.

Then I heard Old Mister Owl say,
"WHO! will take this nasty growl away?
I am not a hound or bear,
I am an owl who flies in the air."

I told him that he was no freak
and then gently kissed his little beak,
I was still his secret friend
we would still play together again.

So what if he were to growl,
he was still Old Mister Owl,
and maybe one happy day
that nasty old growl would go away.

The Little Prince & The Frog

Once upon a silly rhyme
in a past and forgotten time,
there was a prince of sort
who lived in a four story fort.

All the kings horses
and all the kings men,
liked the little prince
and felt he was their friend.

Until late one summer
as the prince romped and roamed,
a frog jumped into his path
and he invited her home.

Well when all the kings horses
and all the kings men,
saw that the little prince
had found himself a new best friend,
they were very angry
and called the prince names.
They didn't want the frog
to join in any royal games.

So the frog leaped away
into the forest wide
because her feelings were hurt
she ran off to hide.

*B*ut that made the prince
lonely and very sad,
for the frog was his best friend,
the best friend he'd ever had.
For days the little prince
searched the forest wide,
hoping to locate the place
where the frog chose to hide.

*H*e looked behind every tree
and under every single rock,
he walked along every stream
and under every single dock.

*B*ut the frog had vanished,
she just could not be found.
It was as if the frog
just up and left town.

*W*hen the King heard
that all the kings men,
used all the kings horses
against the princes' best friend,
he was sad and he was mad
at all of them.
He told them to find the frog
searching everywhere she had been.

*S*o all the kings horses
and all the kings men,
searched for the frog
as the King instructed them.

cont. on next page

The Little Prince & The Frog

*M*eanwhile, the prince grew up
and fell in love with a dear,
for it had been many years
since the frog was near.

*S*o all the kings horses
and all the kings men,
went their own ways
where once they had been.

*A*nd the little prince married
to live under a log,
dwelling happily ever after
with the dear who once was a frog.

Little Looky Lou

Little Looky Lou
looked the whole night through.
She looked to the left and then to the right
She looked and looked with all her might.

She looked down the lane
at the old oak tree
She looked over the hill
towards the deep blue sea.

She looked and looked
all the day long
searching for just one thing
that might go wrong

Little Looky Lou
looking at many and few
Oh No! Look out! Beware
Now she's looking at you!

Old Smokey

Once upon a lion's paw
rests a thorn with-in a claw
And heard within an angry cry
was a hint of a lonesome sigh.

There upon a willow's bend
were the tracks where he had been.
Old Smokey was his name
full of pride and full of fame.

A mighty king once he stood
but now unable to roam as he should,
For deep with-in the lions paw
rested a thorn that I once saw.

With a soft and gentle roar
Old Smokey knocked at my door.
I heard his angry cry, and
saw the thorn that made him cry.

He offered his paw to
my hand
I pulled the thorn and off
he ran
and on the mountains high
he roared a last good bye.

The Little Tree

A poem for you and a poem for me
this is a poem about a little tree
who stood up one day and said, "Hello,
I am a little tree, don't you know".

Well the tree grew to be 10 feet tall
he towered over us cause we were small
and his branches were thick and brown
some very high off the ground.

The little tree stood very tall
but would always bend to the winds call
Back and forth he would sway
time after time and day after day.

I liked that little tree
cause it reminded me of me
free to sway in the gentle breeze
too proud to stand among the other trees.

Old Mr. Donkey Doo

There once was a Donkey
whose name was Doo
He loved to Hee Honk!
For everyone he knew.

He'd hee honk at the cows
and all the other animals too
that's why they called him
Old Mr. Donkey Doo

"Hee Honk! Hee Honk!:
went his morning cry.
"Hee Honk! Hee Honk!"
to everyone passing by.

He's surely a sight to see
that old Mr. Donkey Doo
A hee honking donkey
and he's hee honking just for you.

A Still Small Voice

Once upon a forest tall
I heard a voice so still and small
as the wind, it whistled by
and in its tone I heard a cry.

A sound that beckoned me to come
to come with haste, to run and run.
Should I run to its urgent call
or shall I ignore its cry to fall.

Dash along the beaten path
Hurry and take no rath
Run through the forest tall
to the voice so still and small.

Once upon the forest tall
I answered a voice so still and small
But in the wind that whistles by
was a still small voice that seemed to cry.

Little Old Me

To Bee is not for me.
Who ever wanted to be a bee.?
A bee might want to be.
But he can never be me.

For I am not a Bee
Nor am I a tall oak tree
I am what God meant me to be.
I am just Little Old Me.

Chasing Rainbows

(A True Story)

Let's chase a rainbow
as it bows in the sky
We'll get up real close
just to wonder why?

We'll jump into the car
and zip down the street
Hoping to find the place
where the ground and rainbow meet.

Closer and closer we move
to the end of the bow
For it's touching the road
where we're sure to go.

Suddenly! like a flash
we'll pass through its glow
and watch it shine on the bumper
then the hood and over our window.

Then we'll dash away
always and forever to know
that once upon a time
we were at the end of the rainbow.

The Old Man and His Canoe

There once was an old man
who had a canoe.
He rowed and rowed and never got through.
One stroke for you and one for me,
one for the Owl who slept in the tree.

Onward he goes with a lightning thrust
down memory lane about to bust.
A stroke to the left and one to the right
onward through both the day and night.

He's headed everywhere he has been,
looking for memories lost in the wind.
A stroke to the left and then to the right
onward he goes, passing out of sight.

Mr. Smalley

There once was an old forgotten valley
nestled by a little blue sea.
Where a man lived called Mr. Smalley.

His face was covered with yellow fuzz
Prince of the Little People he was.
And on his feet were tiny little toes
that matched his little turned up nose.

Mr. Smalley with his little feet
ate all the food he could eat.
He didn't like being too small to see
he wanted to be tall like a tree.

So he ate and ate as much as he could
until one day, tall as a tree he stood.
He was tall as he could be.
Now they call him, "Mister Talley"

The Pleasure of a Home

Once upon a mornings dawn,
a little friend of mine was born.
In an open field he gently lay,
without a home or any place to stay.

No warmth or pleasure of a home,
only the fate, forever to roam.
From city to city and town to town,
never to be homeward bound.

How sad to have no home
left to walk in life alone.
As a dog loves his bone,
even a mouse needs a home.

The Better Best

God made us the best of all
said the mountains to the earth
for we are caped with pure white snow
and offer valleys and places for natures birth.

Hold on there partner! Hold on there
sounded the vast desert lands
we are greatest in Gods' sight
teeming with life, above and below our sands.

Nay! Nay! Now here's the Truth
cried the oceans with a mighty roar
for we feed the world its fish,
and are filled with mighty ships and more.

The oceans are the Better Best
they are the very best of all
but the mountains shade the Earth
with great forests that stand up tall.

Yet the desert's blooming landscape
is a breathtaking sight to see
full of cactus, tiny plants, lots of flowers
and even a giant Saguaro tree.

Who is the Better Best?
The greatest of all to see ...
They are all beautiful in God's sight
designed to reveal his love and majesty

Granny Grab Bag

Granny grabbed her bag
and went off to town
Walking to the bus
with an ugly old frown.

"Mr. Bus Driver!" she said,
"you be careful when you drive
watch out for little children
and make sure we arrive alive."

Then she grabbed her bag
and sat in the nearest seat
complaining to all around
about the summer's afternoon heat.

Grumble! Grumble!
I heard her fuss,
as she grabbed her bag
and got off the bus.

Last I knew,
She still was a hag,
that Little Old Lady
we called
Granny Grab Bag.

"Crystal Kitty"

Now hear this story
one told to me
of a cat named Crystal
When she was just a kitty.

She'd run through the house
as fast as she could
then jump on the counter top
that was make out of wood.

She chases any moving light
as though it were a prey,
then off she goes to sleep
for the rest of the day.

She drinks her water
from both bowl and tap,
then curls up in a chair
as though it were my lap.

She's pure white like snow
and as pretty as can be
she's our bundle of joy
and her name is "Crystal Kitty"

The Flaming Star

The star that lights our day,
is but a twinkle in the milky way.
To burn so bright in the sky,
For all to see and wonder why?

Its light is shared so free
with all who dwell on its knee
To twinkle across the heavens far
is the purpose of a flaming star.

From a flicker in the night,
to a burst of brilliant light,
from a distance great and far,
comes the glow of a flaming star.

The Pop Pop of His Corn

Once upon a happy time,
a storyteller told a rhyme.
There were children all around,
but no one spoke or made a sound.

Now the story and the rhyme
was of a long forgotten time.
When a little boy blew his horn
and his daddy made the popcorn.

With a pop and a pop and pop-pop-pop
daddy popped the corn and wouldn't stop.
But the little boy who blew his horn
wouldn't eat his daddy's popcorn.

He just wanted to blow his horn
in the sun, in the rain and even in a storm.
So daddy shared the pop-pop of his corn
with everyone but the boy who played the horn.

The Little Red Hen

There once was a little red hen
who couldn't remember where she had been.
She tried to remember the days events
she even asked for little hints.

Mr. Turkey gobbled at the hen
helping her to remember where she had been,
and Mrs. Cow gave out with a "moo"
but the hen just said "What am I to do?"

Then one night when the moon was full
the hen decided to ask old Mister Bull.
Bravely she climbed the pasture's hill
because the mood of the bull was to kill.

Onward she climbed towards the top
suddenly to come to a very quick stop.
For there before her weary eyes
stood the bull in all his pride.

"Wait! Wait!" cried the little red hen,
"I must know the secret, where have I been?"
"Why that's easy," said the bull to the hen,
"I can tell you where you have been.
Look behind the old oak tree
across the stream to the edge of the sea,
for there my little red hen
is the secret to where you have been."

So with all the secrets of the day
the little red hen went her way,
off to play in a gentle summer wind
now she knows where she had been.

Where do you think the little red hen had been?

A Bear Named Sam

Once upon a story's rhyme
in a long passed forgotten time.
There was a bear whose name was Sam
who ran and ran as fast as he can.

Well Sam belonged to a boy named Bill
who lived on the top of a very high hill.
They always took a morning walk
and Sam would growl as if to talk.

Down the hill they both would go
along the paths that were etched in the snow.
Then across the fields to a little stream
where they both played and slept and dreamed.

Now Sam was a playful bear
he loved to run and sniff the air.
Sam! Bill would gently say
it's time for us to end our play.

So the bear named Sam and his master, Bill
left the stream to climb the very high hill.
For waiting at the top of that hill,
was a hot bath and a meal,
for a boy named Bill.

The Little Duck

Once upon a winter's wonderland
 there was a duck who wouldn't fly away.
Mister Wind said "Please don't stay",
 for the snow was beginning to cover the day.

Fly south cried the Sun
 from this place ... run, run, run.
But Mister Cold laughed and said, "Let him stay ...
 for soon I'll be king over him and the day".

The little duck just wanted to play
 that's why he didn't want to fly away.
But now he must suffer the sorrows of the day
 because he waited too long to fly away.

The moon let out a sorrowful cry
 Oh My! Oh My!
the sun withdrew with a sigh
 Oh My! Oh My!

For the little duck had lost its way,
 only to sleep beneath a frozen bay,
 until the spring shines its light
 when everything will be alright.

A GALAXY FAR AWAY

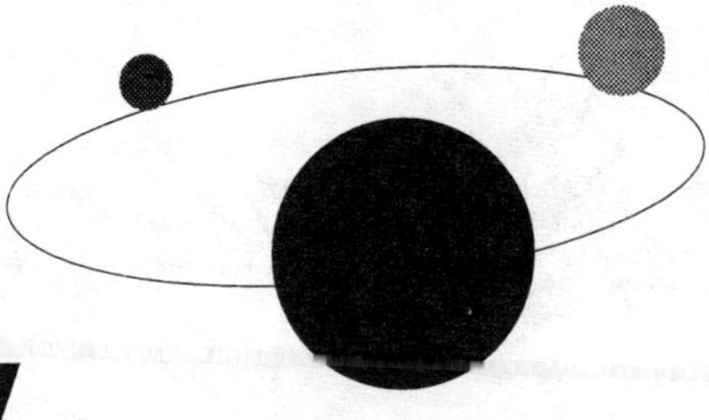

In a galaxy far far away,
a sun will shine to form the day.
Clouds might pass across a golden sky
and mountains quake as if to sigh.
Stars may shine as fires of light,
while the day turns into the night.

In a galaxy far far away,
the wind might blow as it does in May,
and on the other planets there might be
a flood of waters called a sea.
Birds might sing the songs of life,
in a world full of sorrow and strife.

In a galaxy far far away
God's creatures might even pray.

The Fly

Once upon a golden sky,
I came across a tiny fly.
I watched him buzz through the air,
Giving everyone a terrible scare.

Buzz, Buzz zoomed the fly,
he tried to make everyone cry,
around my ear, I heard him zing
as he tried to bite and sting.

So tiny was that little fly
yet he tried to make us cry.
With a swat through the air
I chased him from my hair.

But to my angry surprise
the tiny fly was just too wise.
For up he flew into the air
after someone else to bite and scare.

The Caterpillar

I once saw a caterpillar crawling down the street,
he had so many legs and even more feet.
He was as long as he could be
he was a strange sight to see.

As I watched him crawl away,
I wondered what he did all day.
Does he just crawl around,
can he talk or make a sound?

So I crawled behind him just to see
where he'd go and what he'd be.
For I was curious to know
what he'd do and where he'd go.

All of sudden he began to spin
and guess what happened then.
He spun himself into a web,
I thought, "He must be dead".

But to my surprise,
there before my eyes,
I watched him break that sticky web,
then I knew he wasn't dead.

I just couldn't believe my eyes,
boy what a beautiful surprise,
all those legs and all those feet
no longer crawled down the street.

Like you, I wondered why,
until I saw him begin to fly,
off he flew into the sky,
leaving me to wonder why.

Three Vans in a Row

Three vans traveling all in a row,
only they know where they will go.
For as I see them pass me by,
I wondered where they'll go, and why.

One van is blue with golden flames
filled with people who have no names.
Another is green with an open top
echoing laughter that wouldn't stop.

The third van I could not see
for a truck hid its face from me.
Brown, it seemed, as it passed by
I heard a voice that seemed to cry.

Onward they went into the darkness of night,
guided by their brilliant beams of golden light.
And as I watched them slip away,
I wished I were going their way.

The Girl & The Squirrel

Once upon an evenings' end
a little girl made a new friend.
They played together in the day
as the months passed into the middle of May.

She was a very happy little girl
for she made friends with a baby squirrel.
Through the trees they both would run
just hopping and skipping and having fun.

As the little girl began to grow
and the winter brought the snow,
her new little friend
answered the call of the shifting wind.

Across the brook and down the lane
ran the squirrel without any name.
With a saddened heart and tears in her eyes
the little girl tried to say her last good-byes.

Now she looks toward a future day,
when her little friend will return to play.
Where the snow will melt and flowers bloom
she hopes that day will come very soon.

Three Men and a Bearded Face

Three men and a bearded face
were thrust into an empty timeless space.
They left the earth at a fantastic speed
in search of life's distant seed.

Through the heavens they soared
with rocket like engines that roared.
Onward through empty space
went the three men and a bearded face.

Their destination, the ORION Zone,
where heavenly bodies seemed to groan.
Through the giant black hole
beyond the limits of the human soul.

As the ship soared passed the planet mars
they became children of the stars.
In search of a forgotten kind,
who long ago vanished from time.

Far, far into the depth of space
pass three children of the human race
and one known only as *"the bearded face"*

Consider the Clock

Consider the clock that ticks away the time,
second by second as you read this rhyme.

Listen to the passing of this beautiful day,
see how fast our lives pass away.

Today becomes tomorrow when yesterday is done,
dreams and aspirations become memories undone.

Both joy & sorrow pass through our day,
as though a child had come to play.

There's plenty of time to do our thing,
for in these moments life proudly sings.

But in the day and this very hour.
passes our life as a tiny flower.

Up-up and away goes our soul,
ever passing through time so bold.

Faster and faster goes our day,
onward we march through times array.

Finally we stop as does our times,
to listen as judgement sounds its chimes.

1 2 3 4 5 6 7 8 9 10 11 12

A Story Told

Once upon a story told
in an age when men were bold.
There was a man who sang a song
about a King who did things wrong.

As he sang his scornful tune
he knew his words would be heard soon
But he lived in an age when men were bold
and wasn't afraid to sing of a story told.

Soon his song echoed throughout the town
and in the ears of all who were around.
It told of a King who did things wrong
and many were angry when they heard the song.

For the song that sounded a story told,
spoke of a King who was heartless and cold.
And how the people should not go along
with the King who did things wrong.

Now the man who sang the song
about the King who did things wrong
was filled with great fear
knowing the King was near.

His instincts told him to run and hide,
to seek out another place to abide.
For the words of his song made men blue,
yet they all knew his song was true.

He had sparked anger in the town,
and caused men to stand up and sound.
Yet his heart was raging with fear,
and in his eyes I saw a hint of a tear.

Soon there was fighting in the streets
as they struck out at the soldiers feet.
At first there was only a few,
but the tiny band prospered and grew.

The King who did things wrong,
sent his ships of war against the song.
But the men who fought to be free,
were set on a new life and destiny.

Battle after battle raged in the land,
but the words of the song kept freedom's hand.
And the king who did things wrong,
was overcome by the words of the song.

Many died for the right to be free.
Others began to shape a new destiny.
And the words of that once feared song,
became the law against all who did things wrong.

People of every color and every creed,
joined together to satisfy a common need.
Together they built their cities and their towns,
and today, the words of their song still sounds.

For theirs' is truly a story told
of men through history who were bold.
Men who fought for the right to live and be free,
who died so others could shape their own destiny.

A Greater Story

A greater story was never told,
    than this one told to me.
A story of love, once spoken bold,
    through the cross of Calvary.

He came by water and by blood,
    to bestow God's grace on thee.
He came as a penalty for sin
    to suffer on the cross of Calvary.

God gave his son, a ransomed soul,
    as a gift to set men free.
No greater story was ever told
    than this one told to me.